50 International Cheese Cooking Dishes

By: Kelly Johnson

Table of Contents

- Fondue (Switzerland)
- Queso Fundido (Mexico)
- Macaroni and Cheese (United States)
- Croque Monsieur (France)
- Cheese Soufflé (France)
- Raclette (Switzerland)
- Paneer Butter Masala (India)
- Lasagna (Italy)
- Grilled Cheese Sandwich (United States)
- Mozzarella Sticks (United States)
- Halloumi Fries (Cyprus)
- Chèvre en Croûte (France)
- Feta Cheese Salad (Greece)
- Poutine (Canada)
- Caprese Salad (Italy)
- Empanadas with Cheese (Argentina)
- Baked Brie with Jam (France)
- Cheese Scones (United Kingdom)
- Gnocchi with Gorgonzola Sauce (Italy)
- Ricotta Pancakes (Italy)
- Cheese Blintzes (Poland)
- Parmesan Crusted Chicken (United States)
- Cottage Pie with Cheese Topping (United Kingdom)
- Sarmale with Cheese (Romania)
- Mac and Cheese with Bacon (United States)
- Quesadillas (Mexico)
- Pizza Margherita (Italy)
- Spanakopita (Greece)
- Swiss Cheese and Mushroom Croissants (Switzerland)
- Cheddar Bay Biscuits (United States)
- Raclette with Potatoes (Switzerland)
- Cheese-Stuffed Breads (Turkey)
- Brie and Pear Tart (France)
- Blue Cheese Salad (United States)
- Grilled Halloumi with Pita (Cyprus)

- Beef Wellington with Cheese (United Kingdom)
- Pimento Cheese Dip (United States)
- Cacio e Pepe (Italy)
- Cheese and Chive Biscuits (United States)
- Brie and Cranberry Sandwich (France)
- Cheese Empanadas (Chile)
- Cheddar Cheese Soup (United States)
- Mozzarella in Carrozza (Italy)
- Ricotta and Spinach Stuffed Shells (Italy)
- Queso Blanco Dip (Mexico)
- Frittata with Cheese (Italy)
- Paneer Tikka (India)
- French Onion Soup with Gruyère (France)
- Moussaka with Cheese (Greece)
- Croissant with Ham and Cheese (France)

Fondue (Switzerland)

Ingredients:

- 8 oz Gruyère cheese, shredded
- 8 oz Emmental cheese, shredded
- 1 clove garlic, halved
- 1 cup dry white wine
- 1 tbsp lemon juice
- 1 tbsp cornstarch
- 1 tbsp kirsch (cherry brandy)
- Freshly ground black pepper
- Freshly grated nutmeg
- French bread cubes, for dipping

Instructions:

1. Rub the inside of a fondue pot with the garlic halves.
2. Combine the wine and lemon juice in the pot over medium heat, then gradually add the shredded cheeses, stirring constantly until melted.
3. In a small bowl, mix cornstarch with kirsch and add to the cheese mixture to thicken.
4. Season with freshly ground black pepper and nutmeg.
5. Serve with cubes of French bread for dipping.

Queso Fundido (Mexico)

Ingredients:

- 2 cups Oaxaca cheese, shredded
- 1 cup Chihuahua cheese, shredded
- 1 tbsp olive oil
- 1/2 cup chorizo, crumbled
- 1/2 onion, finely chopped
- 1 jalapeño, finely chopped
- 2 tbsp fresh cilantro, chopped
- Flour tortillas, for serving

Instructions:

1. Heat olive oil in a skillet over medium heat. Add chorizo, onions, and jalapeños. Cook until the chorizo is browned and the vegetables are soft.
2. In a heatproof dish, layer the cheeses and top with the chorizo mixture.
3. Place under a broiler for 2-3 minutes until the cheese is melted and bubbly.
4. Sprinkle with fresh cilantro and serve with warm flour tortillas.

Macaroni and Cheese (United States)

Ingredients:

- 2 cups elbow macaroni
- 2 tbsp butter
- 2 tbsp all-purpose flour
- 2 cups whole milk
- 2 cups shredded sharp cheddar cheese
- 1/2 cup grated Parmesan cheese
- Salt and pepper to taste
- 1/2 tsp paprika (optional)

Instructions:

1. Cook the macaroni according to package instructions, then drain and set aside.
2. In a large saucepan, melt butter over medium heat. Stir in flour and cook for 1-2 minutes.
3. Gradually whisk in milk and cook until the sauce thickens.
4. Stir in cheddar and Parmesan cheese until smooth.
5. Add the cooked macaroni and stir to combine. Season with salt, pepper, and paprika. Serve warm.

Croque Monsieur (France)

Ingredients:

- 4 slices of French bread
- 4 slices of Gruyère cheese
- 4 slices of ham
- 2 tbsp Dijon mustard
- 2 tbsp butter
- 1/2 cup béchamel sauce (see recipe below)
- Salt and pepper to taste

Instructions:

1. Preheat the broiler.
2. Spread mustard on each slice of bread. Layer a slice of ham and a slice of cheese on two of the slices of bread. Top with the other slices of bread.
3. Melt butter in a skillet over medium heat. Toast the sandwiches on both sides until golden brown.
4. Place the sandwiches on a baking sheet, and top with béchamel sauce and additional cheese.
5. Broil for 3-5 minutes, until the cheese is melted and bubbly. Serve immediately.

For Béchamel Sauce:

- 2 tbsp butter
- 2 tbsp flour
- 1 cup milk
- Salt and pepper to taste
- Pinch of nutmeg
1. In a saucepan, melt butter and stir in flour. Gradually add milk while whisking. Cook until thickened, then season with salt, pepper, and nutmeg.

Cheese Soufflé (France)

Ingredients:

- 2 tbsp butter
- 2 tbsp all-purpose flour
- 1 cup whole milk
- 1 ½ cups grated Gruyère cheese
- 4 large eggs, separated
- 1/2 tsp Dijon mustard
- Salt and freshly ground black pepper

Instructions:

1. Preheat the oven to 375°F (190°C). Butter a soufflé dish and sprinkle with grated cheese.
2. In a saucepan, melt butter and stir in flour. Gradually whisk in milk and cook until thickened.
3. Remove from heat, stir in cheese, Dijon mustard, and egg yolks. Season with salt and pepper.
4. Beat egg whites to stiff peaks and gently fold into the cheese mixture.
5. Pour the mixture into the prepared soufflé dish and bake for 25-30 minutes, until puffed and golden. Serve immediately.

Raclette (Switzerland)

Ingredients:

- 1 wedge of raclette cheese
- Small boiled potatoes
- Sliced cured meats (prosciutto, salami)
- Pickles (cornichons)
- Freshly ground black pepper

Instructions:

1. Cut the raclette cheese into thin slices.
2. Heat the cheese in a raclette grill, or melt it in the oven until bubbly and golden.
3. Serve the melted cheese over boiled potatoes, with slices of cured meats and pickles on the side.

Paneer Butter Masala (India)

Ingredients:

- 2 tbsp butter
- 1 large onion, finely chopped
- 2 garlic cloves, minced
- 1 tsp grated ginger
- 1 can (14 oz) crushed tomatoes
- 1 tsp garam masala
- 1 tsp ground cumin
- 1/2 tsp turmeric
- 1/2 cup heavy cream
- 1 block paneer, cubed
- Fresh cilantro for garnish
- Salt to taste

Instructions:

1. Heat butter in a skillet over medium heat. Add onions, garlic, and ginger, cooking until softened.
2. Stir in crushed tomatoes, garam masala, cumin, and turmeric. Simmer for 10 minutes.
3. Add paneer cubes and cook for 5 minutes, allowing the flavors to blend.
4. Stir in heavy cream, and simmer until the sauce thickens.
5. Garnish with cilantro and serve with naan or rice.

Lasagna (Italy)

Ingredients:

- 12 lasagna noodles, cooked
- 1 lb ground beef
- 1 jar marinara sauce
- 1 tbsp olive oil
- 1 onion, chopped
- 2 cloves garlic, minced
- 1 ½ cups ricotta cheese
- 2 cups shredded mozzarella cheese
- 1 cup grated Parmesan cheese
- 1 egg
- Salt and pepper to taste

Instructions:

1. Preheat the oven to 375°F (190°C).
2. Heat olive oil in a pan over medium heat. Add onions and garlic, cooking until softened. Add ground beef and cook until browned. Stir in marinara sauce and season with salt and pepper.
3. In a bowl, combine ricotta cheese, egg, and half of the Parmesan cheese.
4. In a baking dish, spread a layer of meat sauce, followed by lasagna noodles, ricotta mixture, and mozzarella. Repeat layers until all ingredients are used.
5. Top with remaining mozzarella and Parmesan cheese.
6. Cover with foil and bake for 25 minutes. Remove foil and bake for an additional 15 minutes, until bubbly and golden.

Grilled Cheese Sandwich (United States)

Ingredients:

- 2 slices of bread
- 2 slices of cheddar cheese
- 1 tbsp butter

Instructions:

1. Butter one side of each slice of bread.
2. Place one slice of bread, butter-side down, in a skillet over medium heat. Add cheese slices, and top with the second slice of bread, butter-side up.
3. Grill until the bread is golden brown and the cheese is melted, about 3-4 minutes per side.
4. Serve hot.

Mozzarella Sticks (United States)

Ingredients:

- 12 mozzarella sticks (string cheese)
- 1 cup all-purpose flour
- 2 eggs, beaten
- 1 ½ cups breadcrumbs (preferably Italian-style)
- 1 tsp garlic powder
- 1 tsp onion powder
- ½ tsp salt
- ½ tsp pepper
- Vegetable oil for frying
- Marinara sauce, for dipping

Instructions:

1. Freeze the mozzarella sticks for at least 1 hour.
2. In a shallow bowl, combine flour, garlic powder, onion powder, salt, and pepper.
3. Dip each frozen mozzarella stick into the flour mixture, then the beaten eggs, and finally coat with breadcrumbs.
4. Heat vegetable oil in a deep skillet or fryer to 350°F (175°C).
5. Fry the mozzarella sticks for 2-3 minutes until golden and crispy.
6. Drain on paper towels and serve with marinara sauce for dipping.

Halloumi Fries (Cyprus)

Ingredients:

- 1 block halloumi cheese, cut into fries
- 2 tbsp olive oil
- 1 tsp dried oregano
- 1 tsp paprika
- Fresh lemon wedges, for serving
- Fresh parsley, chopped (optional)

Instructions:

1. Heat olive oil in a large frying pan over medium heat.
2. Add the halloumi fries and fry for 2-3 minutes on each side until golden brown.
3. Sprinkle with oregano, paprika, and a pinch of salt.
4. Serve with fresh lemon wedges and garnish with parsley.

Chèvre en Croûte (France)

Ingredients:

- 1 small log of chèvre (goat cheese)
- 1 sheet puff pastry
- 1 tbsp honey
- Fresh thyme, for garnish

Instructions:

1. Preheat the oven to 375°F (190°C).
2. Place the chèvre cheese on a sheet of puff pastry.
3. Drizzle with honey and sprinkle with thyme leaves.
4. Fold the pastry around the cheese, sealing the edges.
5. Place the wrapped cheese on a baking sheet and bake for 20-25 minutes until the pastry is golden and puffed.
6. Let it cool slightly before serving.

Feta Cheese Salad (Greece)

Ingredients:

- 1 cucumber, diced
- 2 tomatoes, diced
- ½ red onion, thinly sliced
- 1 cup Kalamata olives
- ½ cup feta cheese, crumbled
- 2 tbsp olive oil
- 1 tbsp red wine vinegar
- 1 tsp dried oregano
- Salt and pepper to taste

Instructions:

1. In a large bowl, combine the cucumber, tomatoes, red onion, olives, and feta cheese.
2. Drizzle with olive oil and red wine vinegar.
3. Sprinkle with oregano, salt, and pepper.
4. Toss gently to combine and serve chilled.

Poutine (Canada)

Ingredients:

- 4 cups French fries (fried or baked)
- 2 cups cheese curds
- 1 cup beef gravy (or chicken gravy)

Instructions:

1. Prepare the French fries according to your preference (fried or baked).
2. Heat the gravy in a saucepan until warm.
3. Place the fries on a plate and scatter cheese curds evenly over them.
4. Pour the hot gravy over the fries and cheese curds, ensuring they melt slightly.
5. Serve immediately.

Caprese Salad (Italy)

Ingredients:

- 4 large tomatoes, sliced
- 8 oz fresh mozzarella, sliced
- Fresh basil leaves
- 2 tbsp balsamic vinegar
- 3 tbsp olive oil
- Salt and pepper to taste

Instructions:

1. Arrange the tomato slices, mozzarella, and basil leaves alternately on a platter.
2. Drizzle with olive oil and balsamic vinegar.
3. Sprinkle with salt and pepper.
4. Serve immediately as a refreshing appetizer or side dish.

Empanadas with Cheese (Argentina)

Ingredients:

- 1 package empanada dough discs
- 1 ½ cups shredded mozzarella cheese
- ½ cup crumbled queso fresco
- 1 tbsp olive oil
- 1 egg (for egg wash)

Instructions:

1. Preheat the oven to 375°F (190°C).
2. In a bowl, mix the mozzarella, queso fresco, and a pinch of salt.
3. Place a spoonful of the cheese mixture in the center of each empanada dough disc.
4. Fold the dough over to form a half-moon shape and crimp the edges to seal.
5. Brush the tops with beaten egg and place on a baking sheet.
6. Bake for 15-20 minutes until golden and crispy.

Baked Brie with Jam (France)

Ingredients:

- 1 wheel of brie cheese
- 2 tbsp fruit jam (apricot, raspberry, or fig)
- 1 tbsp honey
- 1 tbsp chopped nuts (optional)
- Fresh baguette slices, for serving

Instructions:

1. Preheat the oven to 350°F (175°C).
2. Place the brie wheel on a baking dish and spread the fruit jam on top.
3. Drizzle with honey and sprinkle with chopped nuts (if using).
4. Bake for 10-15 minutes, until the cheese is soft and melted.
5. Serve warm with sliced baguette.

Cheese Scones (United Kingdom)

Ingredients:

- 2 cups all-purpose flour
- 1 tbsp baking powder
- ½ tsp salt
- ½ tsp mustard powder
- 4 tbsp cold butter
- 1 cup grated cheddar cheese
- 1 egg, beaten
- ½ cup milk

Instructions:

1. Preheat the oven to 425°F (220°C).
2. In a bowl, whisk together the flour, baking powder, salt, and mustard powder.
3. Rub the cold butter into the flour mixture until it resembles breadcrumbs.
4. Stir in the grated cheese.
5. Mix the egg and milk together and add to the flour mixture, stirring until a dough forms.
6. Turn the dough onto a floured surface, roll out to 1-inch thick, and cut into rounds.
7. Place the scones on a baking sheet and bake for 10-12 minutes until golden brown.

Gnocchi with Gorgonzola Sauce (Italy)

Ingredients:

- 1 lb gnocchi (store-bought or homemade)
- 1 cup heavy cream
- 4 oz Gorgonzola cheese, crumbled
- 1 tbsp butter
- 1 tbsp olive oil
- 1 clove garlic, minced
- Fresh parsley, chopped for garnish

Instructions:

1. Cook the gnocchi in salted boiling water according to package instructions, then drain.
2. In a skillet, heat butter and olive oil over medium heat. Add the garlic and sauté for 1 minute until fragrant.
3. Add the heavy cream and bring to a simmer.
4. Stir in the Gorgonzola cheese and cook until the sauce thickens.
5. Toss the cooked gnocchi in the sauce until well-coated.
6. Garnish with fresh parsley and serve immediately.

Ricotta Pancakes (Italy)

Ingredients:

- 1 cup ricotta cheese
- 1 cup all-purpose flour
- 1 tbsp sugar
- 1 tsp baking powder
- ½ tsp salt
- 2 eggs
- 1 cup milk
- 1 tsp vanilla extract
- 2 tbsp butter, melted
- Maple syrup or fresh fruit, for serving

Instructions:

1. In a bowl, whisk together the ricotta cheese, eggs, milk, vanilla extract, and melted butter.
2. In another bowl, combine the flour, sugar, baking powder, and salt.
3. Gradually mix the dry ingredients into the wet ingredients until just combined.
4. Heat a griddle or skillet over medium heat and grease with butter or oil.
5. Pour about ¼ cup of the batter onto the skillet and cook for 2-3 minutes per side until golden.
6. Serve with maple syrup or fresh fruit.

Cheese Blintzes (Poland)

Ingredients:

- 8 blintz crepes (store-bought or homemade)
- 1 cup ricotta cheese
- 1 cup farmer's cheese
- 1 egg
- 2 tbsp sugar
- ½ tsp vanilla extract
- 2 tbsp butter

Instructions:

1. In a bowl, combine the ricotta, farmer's cheese, egg, sugar, and vanilla extract.
2. Spoon about 2 tbsp of the cheese mixture into the center of each blintz crepe.
3. Fold the sides of the crepe over the filling and roll up tightly.
4. Heat butter in a pan over medium heat. Fry the filled blintzes for 2-3 minutes per side, until golden brown.
5. Serve with sour cream or fruit preserves.

Parmesan Crusted Chicken (United States)

Ingredients:

- 4 chicken breasts
- 1 cup grated Parmesan cheese
- 1 cup breadcrumbs
- 1 tsp garlic powder
- 1 tsp dried oregano
- 1 egg, beaten
- Salt and pepper to taste
- Olive oil, for frying

Instructions:

1. In a shallow bowl, mix the Parmesan, breadcrumbs, garlic powder, oregano, salt, and pepper.
2. Dip each chicken breast into the beaten egg, then coat with the Parmesan breadcrumb mixture.
3. Heat olive oil in a skillet over medium heat. Fry the chicken breasts for 6-7 minutes per side until golden brown and cooked through.
4. Serve with a side of pasta or salad.

Cottage Pie with Cheese Topping (United Kingdom)

Ingredients:

- 1 lb ground beef or lamb
- 1 onion, chopped
- 2 carrots, chopped
- 1 cup frozen peas
- 1 cup beef broth
- 2 tbsp tomato paste
- 4 cups mashed potatoes
- 1 cup grated cheddar cheese
- 1 tbsp olive oil
- Salt and pepper to taste

Instructions:

1. Heat olive oil in a skillet over medium heat. Cook the onion, carrots, and ground beef until browned.
2. Stir in tomato paste and beef broth. Simmer for 10 minutes until the mixture thickens.
3. Add peas and season with salt and pepper.
4. Spread the meat mixture in a baking dish. Top with mashed potatoes and sprinkle with grated cheddar cheese.
5. Bake in a preheated oven at 375°F (190°C) for 20-25 minutes until the top is golden.

Sarmale with Cheese (Romania)

Ingredients:

- 1 large head of sauerkraut or fresh cabbage
- 1 lb ground pork
- ½ cup rice
- 1 onion, finely chopped
- 1 cup feta cheese, crumbled
- 2 tbsp tomato paste
- 1 tsp thyme
- 1 tsp dill
- Salt and pepper to taste
- 2 cups water or broth

Instructions:

1. Blanch cabbage leaves to soften them, then remove the tough ribs.
2. In a bowl, mix the ground pork, rice, chopped onion, feta cheese, thyme, dill, salt, and pepper.
3. Place a spoonful of the filling in each cabbage leaf and roll tightly.
4. Arrange the rolls in a pot, layering with tomato paste and adding water or broth.
5. Cover and simmer for 1-2 hours until tender. Serve with sour cream.

Mac and Cheese with Bacon (United States)

Ingredients:

- 8 oz elbow macaroni
- 4 slices bacon, chopped
- 2 cups shredded cheddar cheese
- 1 cup milk
- 2 tbsp butter
- 2 tbsp all-purpose flour
- 1 tsp mustard powder
- Salt and pepper to taste

Instructions:

1. Cook the macaroni according to package instructions, then drain.
2. In a skillet, cook the bacon until crispy, then remove and set aside.
3. In a saucepan, melt the butter and whisk in the flour to form a roux. Cook for 1 minute.
4. Gradually whisk in the milk, then stir in the cheddar cheese until melted.
5. Combine the cooked macaroni with the cheese sauce and bacon. Season with mustard powder, salt, and pepper. Serve warm.

Quesadillas (Mexico)

Ingredients:

- 4 flour tortillas
- 2 cups shredded cheese (cheddar, mozzarella, or a mix)
- 1 cup cooked chicken or beef (optional)
- 1 bell pepper, sliced
- 1 small onion, sliced
- 1 tbsp olive oil
- Salsa and sour cream for serving

Instructions:

1. Heat olive oil in a skillet and sauté the bell pepper and onion until softened.
2. Place one tortilla in the skillet over medium heat. Add a generous amount of cheese, sautéed peppers and onions, and cooked meat if desired.
3. Top with another tortilla and cook for 2-3 minutes per side until the cheese is melted and the tortilla is golden brown.
4. Slice into wedges and serve with salsa and sour cream.

Pizza Margherita (Italy)

Ingredients:

- 1 pizza dough (store-bought or homemade)
- 1 cup tomato sauce
- 1 ½ cups fresh mozzarella cheese, sliced
- Fresh basil leaves
- 2 tbsp olive oil
- Salt and pepper to taste

Instructions:

1. Preheat the oven to 475°F (245°C).
2. Roll out the pizza dough and place it on a baking sheet or pizza stone.
3. Spread a thin layer of tomato sauce on the dough.
4. Top with mozzarella slices and bake for 10-12 minutes until the crust is golden.
5. Remove from the oven, drizzle with olive oil, and garnish with fresh basil leaves.

Spanakopita (Greece)

Ingredients:

- 1 package phyllo dough
- 1 lb spinach, chopped
- 1 cup feta cheese, crumbled
- 1 onion, chopped
- 2 eggs, beaten
- ¼ cup olive oil
- Salt and pepper to taste

Instructions:

1. Preheat the oven to 350°F (175°C).
2. Sauté the onion and spinach in olive oil until softened. Let cool.
3. Mix the spinach mixture with feta cheese, eggs, salt, and pepper.
4. Layer several sheets of phyllo dough in a baking dish, brushing each layer with olive oil.
5. Spread the spinach mixture over the phyllo, then top with more phyllo layers.
6. Bake for 30-40 minutes until golden and crispy.

Swiss Cheese and Mushroom Croissants (Switzerland)

Ingredients:

- 1 package croissant dough
- 1 cup Swiss cheese, grated
- 1 cup mushrooms, sliced
- 2 tbsp butter
- 1 tbsp fresh thyme, chopped

Instructions:

1. Preheat the oven to 375°F (190°C).
2. Sauté the mushrooms in butter until tender.
3. Roll out the croissant dough and place cheese and mushrooms in the center of each triangle.
4. Sprinkle with fresh thyme and roll the croissants tightly.
5. Bake for 12-15 minutes until golden and crispy.

Cheddar Bay Biscuits (United States)

Ingredients:

- 2 cups all-purpose flour
- 1 tbsp baking powder
- ½ tsp garlic powder
- 1 tsp salt
- 6 tbsp cold butter, cubed
- 1 ½ cups shredded cheddar cheese
- ¾ cup milk
- 2 tbsp melted butter (for brushing)
- ½ tsp dried parsley

Instructions:

1. Preheat the oven to 450°F (230°C).
2. In a large bowl, mix flour, baking powder, garlic powder, and salt.
3. Cut in the cold butter until the mixture resembles coarse crumbs.
4. Stir in the shredded cheddar cheese and milk until just combined.
5. Drop spoonfuls of dough onto a baking sheet and bake for 10-12 minutes.
6. Brush with melted butter and sprinkle with dried parsley.

Raclette with Potatoes (Switzerland)

Ingredients:

- 1 lb baby potatoes, boiled
- 8 oz raclette cheese, sliced
- 1 tbsp olive oil
- Freshly ground black pepper
- Fresh parsley, chopped (optional)

Instructions:

1. Boil the potatoes in salted water until tender, then drain and set aside.
2. Heat a raclette grill or a regular grill pan.
3. Place the cheese slices on the grill and let them melt until bubbly and golden.
4. Serve the melted cheese over the warm boiled potatoes.
5. Drizzle with olive oil, season with black pepper, and garnish with fresh parsley if desired.

Cheese-Stuffed Breads (Turkey)

Ingredients:

- 2 cups all-purpose flour
- 1 packet active dry yeast
- 1 tsp sugar
- 1 cup warm water
- 1 tbsp olive oil
- 1 tsp salt
- 1 ½ cups feta cheese, crumbled
- 1 tsp dried oregano
- 1 egg, beaten (for egg wash)

Instructions:

1. In a bowl, dissolve the sugar and yeast in warm water. Let it sit for 10 minutes until frothy.
2. Mix the flour, olive oil, and salt in a separate bowl, then add the yeast mixture and knead into a dough.
3. Let the dough rise for 1-1.5 hours until doubled in size.
4. Preheat the oven to 375°F (190°C).
5. Roll out the dough into small rounds, place a spoonful of crumbled feta cheese and oregano in the center of each, and fold the dough over to enclose the filling.
6. Brush the top with beaten egg and bake for 20-25 minutes until golden.

Brie and Pear Tart (France)

Ingredients:

- 1 sheet puff pastry
- 1 small pear, thinly sliced
- 4 oz brie cheese, sliced
- 2 tbsp honey
- 1 tsp fresh thyme, chopped
- 1 tbsp olive oil

Instructions:

1. Preheat the oven to 400°F (200°C).
2. Roll out the puff pastry on a baking sheet.
3. Arrange the sliced pears and brie cheese on the pastry, leaving a small border.
4. Drizzle with honey and sprinkle with fresh thyme.
5. Bake for 20-25 minutes until the pastry is golden and crispy.
6. Drizzle with a little more honey and olive oil before serving.

Blue Cheese Salad (United States)

Ingredients:

- 4 cups mixed greens
- ½ cup blue cheese, crumbled
- ¼ cup walnuts, chopped
- 1 pear, sliced
- 1 tbsp balsamic vinegar
- 2 tbsp olive oil
- Salt and pepper to taste

Instructions:

1. In a large salad bowl, toss the mixed greens with sliced pear and crumbled blue cheese.
2. Drizzle with balsamic vinegar and olive oil.
3. Sprinkle with walnuts and season with salt and pepper.
4. Toss gently and serve immediately.

Grilled Halloumi with Pita (Cyprus)

Ingredients:

- 8 oz halloumi cheese, sliced
- 2 pitas, cut into halves
- 2 tbsp olive oil
- 1 tsp lemon zest
- Fresh mint leaves, for garnish

Instructions:

1. Preheat a grill or grill pan over medium heat.
2. Brush the halloumi slices with olive oil and grill for 2-3 minutes per side until golden brown and slightly crispy.
3. Warm the pita halves on the grill for about 1 minute per side.
4. Serve the grilled halloumi on the pitas, garnished with fresh mint and lemon zest.

Beef Wellington with Cheese (United Kingdom)

Ingredients:

- 1 lb beef tenderloin, trimmed
- 2 tbsp olive oil
- 1 cup mushrooms, finely chopped
- 4 oz brie cheese, sliced
- 1 sheet puff pastry
- 1 egg, beaten (for egg wash)
- Salt and pepper to taste

Instructions:

1. Preheat the oven to 400°F (200°C).
2. Sear the beef tenderloin in olive oil over high heat for 2-3 minutes per side, then season with salt and pepper. Let cool.
3. Sauté the mushrooms until softened and dry. Spread the mushroom mixture over the beef, then layer with brie cheese.
4. Roll the beef in the puff pastry and seal the edges. Brush with beaten egg.
5. Bake for 25-30 minutes until the pastry is golden and crispy.
6. Let rest for 10 minutes before slicing and serving.

Pimento Cheese Dip (United States)

Ingredients:

- 2 cups shredded sharp cheddar cheese
- 1 cup cream cheese, softened
- ½ cup mayonnaise
- ½ cup diced pimentos, drained
- 1 tsp garlic powder
- Salt and pepper to taste

Instructions:

1. In a bowl, mix the shredded cheddar, cream cheese, mayonnaise, and diced pimentos.
2. Add garlic powder, salt, and pepper and stir until well combined.
3. Chill the dip for at least 1 hour before serving. Serve with crackers or vegetables.

Cacio e Pepe (Italy)

Ingredients:

- 8 oz spaghetti or pasta of choice
- 1 cup Pecorino Romano cheese, grated
- 1 tsp black pepper, freshly ground
- 2 tbsp butter
- Salt to taste

Instructions:

1. Cook the pasta in salted boiling water according to package instructions.
2. While the pasta cooks, melt the butter in a pan and add the black pepper. Toast the pepper for 1 minute.
3. Reserve ½ cup of pasta water, then drain the pasta.
4. Toss the pasta in the pan with butter and pepper, adding some reserved pasta water to create a creamy sauce.
5. Stir in the grated Pecorino Romano cheese until creamy and smooth. Serve immediately.

Cheese and Chive Biscuits (United States)

Ingredients:

- 2 cups all-purpose flour
- 1 tbsp baking powder
- ½ tsp salt
- 1 cup shredded cheddar cheese
- 2 tbsp fresh chives, chopped
- 1 cup buttermilk
- ½ cup cold butter, cubed

Instructions:

1. Preheat the oven to 425°F (220°C).
2. In a bowl, mix the flour, baking powder, and salt.
3. Cut in the butter until the mixture resembles coarse crumbs.
4. Stir in the shredded cheddar cheese and chives.
5. Add the buttermilk and stir until just combined.
6. Drop spoonfuls of dough onto a baking sheet and bake for 12-15 minutes until golden.

Brie and Cranberry Sandwich (France)

Ingredients:

- 2 slices French baguette or sourdough bread
- 2 oz brie cheese, sliced
- 2 tbsp cranberry sauce
- Fresh arugula or spinach (optional)

Instructions:

1. Spread cranberry sauce on one slice of bread.
2. Layer with sliced brie cheese and arugula or spinach, if desired.
3. Top with the second slice of bread and serve as is, or toast the sandwich in a pan for 2-3 minutes per side until golden and melty.

Cheese Empanadas (Chile)

Ingredients:

- 2 cups all-purpose flour
- 1/2 cup unsalted butter, chilled and cubed
- 1/4 cup water (or as needed)
- 1 tsp salt
- 1 cup mozzarella cheese, shredded
- 1/2 cup cheddar cheese, shredded
- 1/2 tsp cumin
- 1 egg (for egg wash)

Instructions:

1. In a bowl, combine the flour and salt. Cut in the butter until the mixture resembles coarse crumbs.
2. Slowly add water until a dough forms. Wrap the dough in plastic and chill for 30 minutes.
3. Preheat the oven to 375°F (190°C).
4. Roll out the dough and cut into circles (about 4 inches in diameter).
5. Mix the mozzarella and cheddar cheese with cumin. Place a spoonful of cheese mixture in the center of each dough circle.
6. Fold the dough over to form a half-moon shape and press the edges to seal.
7. Brush with beaten egg and bake for 20-25 minutes, or until golden brown.

Cheddar Cheese Soup (United States)

Ingredients:

- 1 tbsp butter
- 1 small onion, chopped
- 1/4 cup flour
- 2 cups chicken broth
- 2 cups milk
- 3 cups sharp cheddar cheese, shredded
- 1/2 tsp garlic powder
- Salt and pepper to taste
- Crumbled bacon and chives for garnish (optional)

Instructions:

1. In a large pot, melt butter over medium heat. Add chopped onion and cook until softened, about 5 minutes.
2. Stir in the flour and cook for 1-2 minutes, making a roux.
3. Gradually whisk in the chicken broth and milk, bringing to a simmer.
4. Once the soup thickens, add the shredded cheddar cheese and stir until melted.
5. Season with garlic powder, salt, and pepper.
6. Serve with crumbled bacon and chives if desired.

Mozzarella in Carrozza (Italy)

Ingredients:

- 4 slices white bread
- 4 oz mozzarella cheese, sliced
- 2 eggs, beaten
- 1/2 cup flour
- 1/2 cup breadcrumbs
- Olive oil for frying
- Salt and pepper to taste

Instructions:

1. Place a slice of mozzarella between two slices of bread to form a sandwich.
2. In a shallow bowl, beat the eggs. Place flour in one shallow bowl and breadcrumbs in another.
3. Dip the sandwich first in the flour, then in the beaten eggs, and finally coat it with breadcrumbs.
4. Heat olive oil in a pan over medium heat. Fry the sandwiches for 3-4 minutes on each side, or until golden and crispy.
5. Season with salt and pepper before serving.

Ricotta and Spinach Stuffed Shells (Italy)

Ingredients:

- 12 jumbo pasta shells
- 1 cup ricotta cheese
- 1 cup mozzarella cheese, shredded
- 1/2 cup Parmesan cheese, grated
- 1 cup spinach, cooked and chopped
- 1 egg
- 2 cups marinara sauce
- Salt and pepper to taste

Instructions:

1. Preheat the oven to 375°F (190°C).
2. Cook the jumbo shells according to package instructions, then drain and set aside.
3. In a bowl, mix ricotta, mozzarella, Parmesan, spinach, and egg. Season with salt and pepper.
4. Stuff each pasta shell with the cheese and spinach mixture.
5. Spread a thin layer of marinara sauce in a baking dish. Arrange the stuffed shells on top and cover with remaining marinara sauce.
6. Cover with foil and bake for 25 minutes. Remove the foil and bake for an additional 10 minutes, until bubbly and golden.

Queso Blanco Dip (Mexico)

Ingredients:

- 1 tbsp butter
- 1/4 cup onion, chopped
- 1/4 cup green chilies, chopped
- 1 1/2 cups white cheddar cheese, shredded
- 1/2 cup Monterey Jack cheese, shredded
- 1/2 cup milk
- 1 tbsp cornstarch (optional, for thicker dip)
- Salt to taste

Instructions:

1. In a saucepan, melt butter over medium heat. Add the chopped onion and green chilies, and cook until softened.
2. Stir in the shredded cheeses and milk, and cook, stirring frequently, until the cheese is melted and the dip is smooth.
3. If you prefer a thicker consistency, dissolve the cornstarch in a small amount of water and add it to the dip, stirring until thickened.
4. Season with salt to taste and serve warm with tortilla chips or fresh vegetables.

Frittata with Cheese (Italy)

Ingredients:

- 6 large eggs
- 1/4 cup milk
- 1/2 cup mozzarella cheese, shredded
- 1/4 cup Parmesan cheese, grated
- 1/2 cup spinach, chopped
- 1/2 cup bell peppers, diced
- 1 small onion, diced
- Salt and pepper to taste
- 1 tbsp olive oil

Instructions:

1. Preheat the oven to 350°F (175°C).
2. In a bowl, whisk the eggs and milk until well combined. Stir in the mozzarella, Parmesan, spinach, bell peppers, and onion. Season with salt and pepper.
3. Heat olive oil in a skillet over medium heat. Pour in the egg mixture and cook for 2-3 minutes, allowing the edges to set.
4. Transfer the skillet to the oven and bake for 15-20 minutes, or until the center is set and the top is golden.
5. Slice and serve warm.

Paneer Tikka (India)

Ingredients:

- 1 lb paneer, cubed
- 1/4 cup yogurt
- 1 tbsp lemon juice
- 1 tbsp ginger-garlic paste
- 1 tbsp garam masala
- 1 tsp turmeric powder
- 1 tsp red chili powder
- 1/2 tsp cumin powder
- Salt to taste
- 1 tbsp oil
- Fresh cilantro for garnish

Instructions:

1. In a bowl, combine the yogurt, lemon juice, ginger-garlic paste, garam masala, turmeric, red chili powder, cumin, salt, and oil to make a marinade.
2. Add the paneer cubes to the marinade and coat well. Let it marinate for at least 30 minutes.
3. Preheat the grill or oven to 400°F (200°C).
4. Thread the marinated paneer onto skewers and place them on the grill or in the oven. Cook for 15-20 minutes, basting occasionally with the marinade.
5. Garnish with fresh cilantro and serve with naan or rice.

French Onion Soup with Gruyère (France)

Ingredients:

- 4 large onions, thinly sliced
- 4 tbsp butter
- 1 tbsp olive oil
- 1 tsp sugar
- 2 cloves garlic, minced
- 6 cups beef broth
- 1/2 cup white wine (optional)
- 1 bay leaf
- 1/2 tsp thyme
- Salt and pepper to taste
- 1 baguette, sliced
- 2 cups Gruyère cheese, grated

Instructions:

1. In a large pot, melt butter and olive oil over medium heat. Add onions and sugar, cooking until the onions are caramelized and golden brown (about 25 minutes).
2. Add the garlic and cook for 1 more minute.
3. Pour in the wine (if using) and scrape the browned bits from the bottom of the pot. Add the beef broth, bay leaf, thyme, salt, and pepper.
4. Bring to a simmer and cook for 20 minutes.
5. Preheat the broiler. Ladle the soup into oven-safe bowls, top with a slice of baguette, and sprinkle generously with Gruyère cheese.
6. Broil the bowls until the cheese is melted and bubbly, about 2-3 minutes. Serve hot.

Moussaka with Cheese (Greece)

Ingredients:

- 2 medium eggplants, sliced into 1/2-inch rounds
- 1 lb ground beef or lamb
- 1 onion, chopped
- 2 cloves garlic, minced
- 1 can (14 oz) crushed tomatoes
- 1/4 cup red wine (optional)
- 1 tsp cinnamon
- 1/2 tsp oregano
- Salt and pepper to taste
- 1/2 cup béchamel sauce (see below)
- 1/2 cup feta cheese, crumbled
- 1/4 cup Parmesan cheese, grated

For Béchamel Sauce:

- 2 tbsp butter
- 2 tbsp flour
- 1 cup milk
- 1/4 cup Parmesan cheese
- Salt and pepper to taste

Instructions:

1. Preheat the oven to 375°F (190°C).
2. Salt the eggplant slices and let them sit for 10 minutes to draw out excess moisture. Pat them dry with paper towels.
3. Heat olive oil in a skillet and fry the eggplant slices until golden brown, then set aside.
4. In the same skillet, brown the ground meat with the onion and garlic. Add the crushed tomatoes, red wine, cinnamon, oregano, salt, and pepper. Simmer for 15-20 minutes.
5. For the béchamel sauce, melt butter in a saucepan, stir in flour to make a roux, then gradually add the milk, whisking until thickened. Remove from heat and stir in Parmesan.
6. In a baking dish, layer the eggplant, then the meat mixture, and then the béchamel sauce. Repeat the layers, finishing with the béchamel on top.

7. Sprinkle the top with feta and Parmesan cheese, then bake for 30-40 minutes, until golden.

Croissant with Ham and Cheese (France)

Ingredients:

- 4 croissants (fresh or day-old)
- 4 slices ham
- 4 slices Swiss cheese (or Gruyère)
- 1 tbsp Dijon mustard (optional)
- 1 tbsp butter

Instructions:

1. Preheat the oven to 375°F (190°C).
2. Slice the croissants in half horizontally.
3. Spread Dijon mustard on the inside of each croissant (optional).
4. Place a slice of ham and cheese inside each croissant.
5. Place the croissants on a baking sheet and bake for 10-12 minutes, or until the cheese is melted and the croissants are golden.
6. Serve warm with a side of salad or pickles.

www.ingramcontent.com/pod-product-compliance
Lightning Source LLC
LaVergne TN
LVHW081326060526
838201LV00055B/2480